WASHINGTON
The Nation's Capital

WASHINGTON
The Nation's Capital

Rupert O. Matthews

MALLARD
PRESS

MALLARD PRESS
An imprint of
BDD Promotional Book Company, Inc.
666 Fifth Avenue
New York, N.Y. 10103

Mallard Press and its accompanying design
and logo are trademarks of
BDD Promotional Book Company, Inc.

First published in the United States of America
in 1990 by Mallard Press.

Printed and Bound in Spain.

ISBN 0-792-45096-5

Produced by Ted Smart
Text by Rupert O. Matthews
Design by Sara Cooper

**The Photographs in this book appear courtesy of
Uniphoto Picture Agency**

Facing page: The colonnade of the Jefferson Memorial. Built in 1943 to commemorate the work of Thomas Jefferson, the Memorial embodies much of which Jefferson was proud. The circular design, topped by a dome is typical of the architectural style which Jefferson favored. He even placed a dome on top of his house at Monticello. Left: The great dome of the Capitol, completed during the course of the Civil War by President Lincoln who was anxious to show that he believed the Union would survive. Continuing to spend public money on the meeting house of the Union was a most effective way of stating this belief for all to see. Overleaf: The impressive steps leading to the Supreme Court. The building was completed in 1935 after the Judges of the Supreme Court found their previous quarters in the Capitol becoming rather cramped.

If any city on earth deserves the title of national capital, it is Washington D.C. Before the United States came into being as a nation, Washington did not exist as a city. It was born with the nation, being the creation of the great men who brought the nation through its birthpains and gave it form. The city grew with the nation, expanding as new states joined the union and swelling to perform its increasing governmental function.

Today it is a city of four million inhabitants which plays host to 19 million visitors each year. But most important of all it is the capital. It contains the great offices of state, the public buildings to contain them and the national monuments to heroes of the past. Unlike the capitals of many other countries, Washington was built to be the capital, the city of government free from industry and commerce.

The story of Washington began on 4th July 1776, together with the story of the United States. On that date the thirteen colonies declared themselves to be independent of Britain. The new union would inevitably need both a constitution and a capital, but both had to wait some years, for the British were not willing to lose their American colonies without a struggle. Before the nation's capital could be built, the nation had to free itself.

In June 1777 a large British army marched south from Canada under the command of General Burgoyne with the intention of moving down the Hudson to link up with an

army under General Howe in New York, and so split the fledgling nation in two. Defeating an American force at Ticonderoga, Burgoyne marched on to Saratoga where he met an American army under General Gates and was utterly defeated. Cut off from Canada, Burgoyne surrendered his entire force.

With the victory, the whole course of the war changed. The British fell back on to the defensive while other countries began to take the new United States seriously. The French King Louis XVI, always willing to embarrass the British, lent the colonists vital help. Under the inspiring

Above and facing page: The Chesapeake and Ohio Canal, which is now a National Historical Park used chiefly for the recreation of Washington citizens. When it was built in the 1800s the canal was intended to have served as a vital industrial routeway, linking Chesapeake Bay to the interior waterways. Within only a few years, however, it was superceded by the more competitive railroads and ceased functioning. Right and far right: The quiet streets of Georgetown. Originally a small town which existed long before the Government decided to build Washington City, Georgetown is now a famous shopping district with branches of the nation's most exclusive stores rubbing shoulders with European outlets and small independent shops.

The Congressmen locked the doors and waited for the soldiers to go home. Soon afterwards the Congress decided that it needed a special city where it could meet free from interference. The idea of Washington D.C. was born.

The idea was not put into practice quickly due to disagreements within Congress. It was generally assumed that a thriving commercial center would develop wherever the national capital was placed. As a result several cities put themselves forward as capitals and congressmen from northern and southern states insisted that the capital should lie within their areas. The rivalry was made worse by other wrangles between North and South.

Finally, in 1790, the New Yorker Alexander Hamilton met with Thomas Jefferson of Virginia in an attempt to reach some sort of agreement. Over dinner in a New York restaurant the two men came to an arrangement. Hamilton agreed to support a southern site for the capital in return for Jefferson's promise that the southern states would help pay the war debts incurred by the northern states. Fortunately both men were able to persuade their respective followers to back the plan.

Under the new Constitution, signed in 1787, George Washington was elected the first President of the United States. Congress authorized him to choose a site for the new capital on the banks of the Potomac River, on the borders between Maryland and Virginia. It was an apt choice of site for the name Potomac, or Potowmack as it was then spelt, means 'River of the Meeting of the Tribes'.

Washington, himself a surveyor, chose a site at the confluence of the Potomac and the Eastern Branch which included land of both states. Washington chose his site well as the present face of the city shows, but the early history of the enterprise was to be troublesome in the extreme.

At this time the future site of Washington was taken up

leadership of George Washington, the Americans gradually defeated the numerically superior British forces until at Yorktown, in 1781, General Cornwallis was forced to surrender the main British army. Two years later a peace treaty was signed.

The Continental Congress met in the State House in Philadelphia to organize the newly free states and to decide on a form of government. One thing they omitted to do, however, was to pay the backpay of the soldiers who had won the very independence they discussed. The soldiers marched on Congress and surged around the State House.

by farms and was in private ownership. Eager not to trample on the very liberties which they had fought to defend, the Congressmen devised a plan which they hoped would satisfy the owners and make them agree to the building of a national capital on their land. It was proposed that land required for public buildings would be bought by the government for $66.66 an acre, a fairly generous price for the time. Land needed for roads and thoroughfares was to be handed over free.

The big incentive to the farmers and landowners was that they would be free to sell all other land themselves, so long

as the lots fitted in with the street plan decided on by the government. The owners knew that prices for building plots in a national capital would be far higher than either the value of farmland or the $66.66 offered by the government. Proceeds from these sales were to be divided equally between the government and the owners. The owners eagerly accepted, expecting to make a quick and easy fortune, while the government expected to raise enough money to pay for the public buildings.

Having secured the agreement of the residents to hand over the land necessary for the capital, Congress had to decide on a plan for the city. On the recommendation of President Washington the 37 year old Frenchman Major Pierre Charles L'Enfant was appointed to draw up plans. L'Enfant was, by profession, a military engineer and was one of many Frenchmen who joined the American Revolutionary Army in the wake of Saratoga. He had served with distinction and had come to the notice of Washington. After the war ended L'Enfant did not follow the lead of many of his compatriots in returning to Europe. Instead he stayed in America as an architect designing, among other structures, New York City Hall.

As a military engineer, L'Enfant needed a good eye for ground so that he could take advantage of even the slightest

rise or dip for defensive purposes. Taking up his appointment, L'Enfant journeyed to the site on the banks of the Potomac and began strolling through the orchards and fields, eyeing up the hills and valleys. He had only a few months to produce a street plan and layout for the future capital.

The task was not as daunting as it might seem. L'Enfant had been born in Paris, one of Europe's major capital cities, and knew it well. He borrowed maps and plans of other cities including Milan, Amsterdam, Turin, Frankfurt and Bordeaux. By studying existing towns and how they worked, L'Enfant hoped that 'the contemplation of what exists may serve to suggest a variety of new ideas.'

But L'Enfant had a clear model close at hand in the shape of Williamsburg, capital of Virginia. The large cities of Europe which L'Enfant was studying were ancient industrial or mercantile centers which had grown up over many centuries and where government was only an incidental function. Williamsburg, by contrast, had been designed and built as a city for government.

Early colonial Virginia was founded on the tobacco trade. Plantations were strung out along the many rivers and inlets of the colony, up which ships sailed to collect the tobacco and unload cargoes from Britain. There had been no need for a town or port larger than a single wharf, so none had emerged. When, in 1698, the colony was granted limited self-government there was no obvious site for the capital, so one was built.

Williamsburg was designed around a central truncated T-shaped crossing of main streets. Duke of Gloucester Street was a broad avenue with at one end the College and the Capitol at the other. The Governor's Palace stood at the head of a second avenue running at right angles to Duke of Gloucester Street. The surrounding area was filled with residential streets where the landowners of Virginia built sumptuous townhouses. The city was a great success. Whenever the Virginian Assembly was in session the landowners moved to their townhouses, together with their families and servants. A theatre, the first in British America, was opened and Williamsburg soon became the center of 'society.'

No doubt L'Enfant hoped to repeat the success of Williamsburg. The eventual plans he produced drew much inspiration from Williamsburg and from Paris, though some features were wholly original.

In planning Washington, L'Enfant had in mind the

concept of a magnificent city which, for beauty and elegance, would far surpass any other on Earth. He wrote that 'The positions for the different edifices, and for the several squares, were first determined on the most advantageous ground, commanding the most extensive prospects.' He explained the street plan by stating that 'avenues of direct communication have been devised to preserve through the whole a reciprocity of sight at the same time attention has been paid to the passing of those leading avenues over the most favorable ground for prospect and convenience.' It is revealing that L'Enfant placed convenience second to visual impression.

The center of the city was to be dominated by a truncated T-shape of main streets, like Williamsburg. The longer street, The Mall was to lead from the Capitol to the Potomac, while the Presidential Palace was to close the shorter arm. Around this central core L'Enfant envisaged a town of regular grid pattern with north-south streets identified by numbers and east-west streets by letters. Long diagonal streets, named after the states of the Union, were to cut across the grid so as to make travel across town easier. Concerned with the visual appearance of a project which L'Enfant increasingly saw as 'his' city, he decreed that the main avenues should be 160 feet wide and consist of carriageways flanked by tree-shaded pathways. The ordinary grid-pattern streets were to be 90 feet wide. All

Facing page top: The Chesapeake and Ohio Canal passes through wooded country some miles north of Georgetown where it is enjoyed by picnickers and joggers alike. Facing page bottom: The 184 mile long canal is now a National Historical Park and is staffed by rangers. During the summer months the rangers dress in early 19th century styles and run traditional mule-drawn canal barges along the waterway. The bargees entertain their passengers with old folk songs and with stories of the canal's history. Left: The canal in Georgetown, where it is lined with town houses. The water is kept moving in the winter to prevent ice from building up to a point when it might damage the lock machinery. Overleaf: A view across Washington from the northwest at dawn.

this at a time when in European capitals a street 50 feet wide was considered to be a major thoroughfare.

The plan was revealed in 1792 amid universal acclamation, and even today it is considered by many architects to be the finest city plan ever devised. Unfortunately the plan ran into immediate trouble. The landowners, led by the influential Daniel Carroll, objected violently. They had agreed to hand over land for roads free of charge and felt that the extremely wide streets planned by L'Enfant were robbing them of land, and therefore money. The senior surveyor, Andrew Ellicot, joined the controversy when he claimed L'Enfant had refused to work with him and had ignored all his advice and proposals.

George Washington stepped in to support L'Enfant. The Frenchman had, after all, produced a marvellous plan in a short period of time and his imperious manner could be excused on the grounds that he was used to army work where his orders were immediately put into effect by subordinates. The storm subsided, and L'Enfant began laying plans for the public buildings. He declared the slight rise known as Jenkins Hill to be 'a pedestal waiting for a monument' and began making plans for the construction of the Capitol on the site.

At this point disaster struck for L'Enfant. Daniel Carroll decided that he would not sell all his land, but would keep back a small plot as the site for a new home for himself in the national capital. When L'Enfant heard that Carroll's workmen had begun work on the house he was furious that anyone would upset his plans. L'Enfant sent in his own team of workmen and had the half-completed structure

The National Air and Space Museum stands on the Mall beside 7th Avenue. It contains many hundreds of exhibits, including the Wright Brothers' original Kittihawk aircraft and also pieces of moonrock. There are recreations of famous moments in the history of flight and space travel, such as the planting of the first United States flag on the Moon. Films play day-long in the attached Langley Theater on a 50 foot high screen. These features have established the museum as the most visited in Washington. But the establishment is far more than a tourist attraction. It also houses a huge library of historical aeronautical works which are available to research workers and has a fine art collection.

torn down. This time the temperamental Frenchman had gone too far.

Carroll pulled all the political strings he could, and as a wealthy landowner related to several government men he had many to pull. Even so his fury might have proved ineffectual if George Washington had stood by his appointee. But Washington himself was tiring of L'Enfant who consistently refused to reveal details of his plans. 'I did not expect to meet with such perverseness in Major L'Enfant,

as his late conduct exhibited', wrote Washington refusing to lend his support to the Frenchman any further.

A few days later L'Enfant received a short, curt note from the Commissioners appointed to oversee construction work. After a few polite preambles it read 'We have been notified that we are no longer to consider you as engaged in the business of the federal City.'

It was a terrible blow to L'Enfant who considered that the creation of the city was the great work of his life. The

Congress offered him 500 guineas, the new nation was still using English money at this point, and a plot of land in the capital. L'Enfant refused both and sued the government for the massive sum of 18,000 guineas. He lost his case and slid into poverty.

For several years L'Enfant trailed around Washington in the hope of gaining recognition from the bureaucracy or the government. His gaunt figure, accompanied by his faithful dog, became a familiar sight on the developing avenues and streets he had designed. Dressed in his old, but still serviceable blue army coat and a bell-crowned beaver hat he stalked the streets swinging a formidable hickory cane and carrying a bundle of documents relating to his case. But he gained nothing except sympathy from men powerless to act. Those able to help him either refused to see him or brushed him off with excuses.

Much of this official disdain was due to Thomas Jefferson. Often described as a genius himself, Jefferson took an instant and violent dislike to the architectural genius of L'Enfant. From 1796 as Vice-President and from 1801 as President, Jefferson continually blocked any moves to reward L'Enfant. The reasons for this feud are difficult to pin down, but one contemporary ascribed it to L'Enfant's membership of the Society of Cincinnatti, a gathering of eminent men from which Jefferson was excluded.

Jefferson stepped down from the Presidency in 1809 and almost at once L'Enfant's efforts began to bear fruit. On 1st May 1810 Congress granted him the sum of $1,394.20. This corresponded to the original offer of 500 guineas converted into new United States dollars plus the interest it would have earned over the intervening years. Realizing that this was all he could expect, L'Enfant accepted the gift and then retired from public life to live on his meagre investments and the charity of friends. He died in virtual poverty and complete obscurity on 14th June 1825.

The city he had planned, meanwhile, continued to grow and flourish as if it had taken on a life of its own. The surveyor who had acted as L'Enfant's draughtsman, Andrew Ellicott, was told to 'Prepare a new plan (of the city) for publication using material gathered and information acquired while acting surveyor.' Ellicott tidied up

some unclear details on L'Enfant's map and made a few minor alterations. His new map was then handed over to a printer who began striking off copies in October 1792. L'Enfant was one of the first customers at the printers. When he saw that Ellicott had virtually copied his plans, but without acknowledging the fact, L'Enfant flew into a fury and stormed out of the office.

The printed map was circulated widely in the hope of tempting builders and developers into investing in the city. It was also passed to the Commissioners who ordered

These pages: Mount Vernon, home of George Washington. The house is very much Washington's own creation. He inherited the property in 1761 when it was a simple cottage with some attached tobacco fields. He gradually built the plantation up to include 8,000 acres and enlarged the house to its present size. Washington was a student of European architecture and completed Mount Vernon on the fashionable Palladian plan with two sweeping, curved wings containing the domestic quarters. It was Mount Vernon which Washington left to take up the command of the army during the War of Independence and to Mount Vernon he returned after his second term in office.

ground to subordinates and left the Federal City and did not return until December. The Commissioners were not amused at being treated in this way. On 23rd December they met and noted in their records 'Major Ellicott after his absence returned to us in the winter, we do not accept his farther service. The business we believe was going on full as well without him.' Not much of a Christmas present for Andrew Ellicott. He was, however, a capable man and went on to enjoy a prosperous career as a surveyor and mathematician.

Fresh troubles were soon to appear. There were now three versions of the street plan of the new Federal Capital. L'Enfant's plan had been issued in small numbers, Ellicott's map had experienced a large print run and the Commissioners held a third, updated map which they kept to themselves. When developers, tempted by the thought of erecting fine houses or hotels in advantageous positions, approached the Commissioners they were very often informed they could not build where they wanted to. The builders pointed out the plot on their maps, invariably printed from Ellicott's work. But the Commissioners stated that such a plot did not exist on their new, and unrevealed, map.

Bitter legal wrangles developed with clients believing they were being cheated and the Commissioners stating that they knew best. The presence of two public and one private map caused endless confusions. Finally, on 8th April 1802, the House of Representatives passed a motion forcing the Commissioners to print their more accurate, but less accessible map. Only then did the public get to see the exact shape of their capital city.

Meanwhile, back in 1792 when Ellicott was dismissed, the Commissioners knew that it had been decided that the

Ellicott to lay out the roads and building plots on the ground using markers and stakes. He went to work, but soon ran into problems. The original land survey had not been as accurate as it might have been. Where Ellicott had confidently planned a residential square on dry ground, he found a swampy mass of reeds and rushes. He made some hasty changes to the map held by the Commissioners and continued work. More unexpected swamps and hills were found and further changes made.

In the summer of 1793 Ellicott received an offer for a better paid task. He handed the chore of staking out the

government would move from its temporary home in Philadelphia to Washington in the year 1800. At least some of the public buildings needed to be completed by then. Congress therefore declared a competition for the design of the Presidential Palace and put up a prize of $500. The plan submitted by James Hoban, an Irishman living in Charleston, was accepted and work began almost at once, the first stone being laid in 1792. As originally built the Presidential Palace was an elegant mansion reminiscent of the Irish country houses with which Hoban would have been familiar in his youth. The building was originally a

four-sided house with elegant pilasters and a Classical pediment facing the Ellipse and looking towards The Mall.

The exterior of the building has been changed many times since. The first major alteration came in 1824 when the triangular pediment and its Ionic pilasters were replaced with the South Portico by the architect Benjamin Latrobe. Five years later President Jackson added the North Portico to balance the plan of the building.

By 1948 the White House, as the Presidential Palace was

radical alterations as the exterior, but the changes it has seen have been far more numerous. When President John Adams, the first to take up residence in the Presidential Palace, arrived the building was incomplete. His wife, the intelligent and popular Abigail, was forced to hang the laundry in the unfinished East Room, supposedly one of the prestige state rooms.

Until 1902 the general public was free to enter the White House at any time and to wander freely through the state

The town of Alexandria, Virginia, was originally included in the Federal District but was later handed back to Virginia when it appeared the national capital would not be needing the land south of the Potomac. Today it is a mix of charming 18th century town houses and bustling modern city. Above: The New Wolf Trap Building, a center for the performing arts. Right: The 300 foot tower of the George Washington Masonic National Memorial which commemorates Washington's leading role in the Masonic movement. Facing page top: An elegant square in Alexandria. Facing page bottom: A typical brick street of Alexandria's old town.

by then known, was in a serious state of disrepair. President Truman even began to worry that the bathtub would fall through to the floor beneath. The sum of $6 million was spent on renovations, and on building a balcony within the South Portico at the level of the upstairs rooms. Though today the balcony is an accepted part of the building, it caused a storm of controversy when first installed. There are still people who believe that the White House had a more graceful appearance without the balcony.

The interior of the White House has not undergone such

rooms. Since that date, however, the building is open for only two hours each day and is closed entirely when state occasions are taking place. The rooms the visitors see have been redecorated and refurbished many times since they were first built for the Presidential family are free to impress their personality on their home. However, the layout of the various rooms, especially those used for government business, have changed little.

The largest chamber is the East Room which is generally used as the audience chamber where the presidents

competition was merely a matter of form and that his design would be accepted. He therefore went ahead to produce complete plans.

However, among the plans submitted to the competition were those of Dr William Thornton, an amateur architect. These, according to President Washington, were perfect in 'the grandeur, simplicity, and beauty of the exterior; the propriety with which the apartments are distributed, and economy in the whole mass of the structure.'

Washington wasted little time in letting the Commissioners know they were to follow Thornton's plans, which gave them a problem. They now had two architects who

had both been promised the contract and the prize. They decided on a disastrous compromise. Thornton was to be awarded the prize, but Hallet was given the task of building the structure. It would appear that the Commissioners felt that they owed Hallet a great deal and wished to repay him through this appointment.

Almost at once Hallet began making difficulties, declaring that Thornton's amateur plans were unworkable. He produced his own plans, ostensibly a reworking of Thornton's but in reality very different from the amateur's ideas. The new plans were, however, much cheaper to implement than the original and so were approved. Hallet could not

resist the temptation to further alter Thornton's plans without actually telling anyone what he was doing.

Nevertheless, 18th September 1793 saw the ceremony of laying the cornerstone, and a very impressive ceremony it was too. Because the ceremony involved stone laying it was decided to incorporate the Freemason Lodges of the new nation in the formalities, after all George Washington was a leading Freemason himself. A contemporary described it as 'one of the grandest masonic processions which, perhaps, ever was exhibited on the like important occasion.'

The grand procession began at 10 o'clock in the morning when George Washington crossed the Potomac from the south. A troop of artillery fired a salute to the President, who was welcomed by members of Maryland Lodge No. 9 and Virginia Lodge No. 22 Freemasons. Together with the artillery and the two lodges, President Washington marched to President's Square. There the final procession was put in order, consisting of surveyors, the Mayor of Georgetown, the artillery, the Commissioners, representative workmen, various grades of Freemason, sword bearers and finally the President.

Arriving at the site of the Capitol, the procession spread out to form a vast hollow square around the foundation site. While the assembled masses stood in 'silent awful order', Washington ceremonially tapped the stone in place and secured on it a silver plaque which was engraved with

the following words.

'This southeast corner stone of the Capitol of the United States of America, in the city of Washington was laid on the 18th., day of September, 1793, in the eighteenth year of American Independence, in the first year of the second term of the presidency of George Washington, whose virtues in the civil administration of his country have been as conspicuous and beneficial as his military valor and prudence have been useful in establishing her liberties, and in the year of Masonry 5793, by the President of the United States, in concert with the Grand Lodge of Maryland, several lodges under its jurisdiction, and Lodge No. 22, from Alexandria, VA.; Thomas F. Johnson, David Steuart, and Daniel Carroll, Commissioners; Joseph Clark, Right Worshipful Grand Master, pro tempore; James Hoban and Stephan Hallette, architects; Collin Williamson, master mason.'

The entire procession then retired to a large marquee where a 500lb ox had been roasting on a spit.

After such a grand beginning the early history of the Capitol is rather disappointing. Hallet began building the Capitol to his new revised plans, but it was not long before George Washington noticed that the structure rising from Capitol Hill bore little relation to the plans which had been approved. In June 1794 Hallet was dismissed. A few months later Dr Thornton was appointed to be one of the Commissioners of the Capital and was given responsibility for the Capitol.

Early in 1795 American officials in London signed up George Hadfield to continue the work. Hadfield was a brilliant young architectural student who had passed all the tests set by the Royal Academy with ease. He arrived in Washington in October to find the foundations completed and the walls complete to a height of around three feet.

Facing page and left: The statue of General Andrew Jackson, surrounded by cannon which he captured at the Battle of Pensacola, which was the first equestrian statue made in the United States. Above: The White House.

complete. But that is more than could have been said for the rest of the city.

Like the major public buildings the rest of the city was progressing only slowly. The street plan, which was a slightly modified version of L'Enfant's original scheme, allowed for large numbers of houses to be erected on the grid streets and along the diagonal avenues. The land was accordingly divided up into suitably sized plots and offered for sale. Few people were interested. Congressmen did not want to risk buying land or building a house when they might not be returned at the next elections, states were reluctant to buy property for their representatives and the

sales moving the Commissioners agreed to the new deal.

Unfortunately the two men had secured a near monopoly on land around the principal public buildings and demanded highly inflated prices. Consequently few people bought any lots and the expected houses, taverns and theatres failed to materialize. What facilities did exist were in Georgetown to the northwest over Rock Creek and beyond the range of the Greenleaf-Morris property deal. Congressmen and state employees were forced to find what lodgings they could. Many were had to 'live like scholars in a college or monks in a monastery, crowded ten or twenty to a house and otherwise secluded from society.'

The White House is built of a pleasantly colored sandstone and originally blended in well with the surrounding countryside which then reached right to its grounds. It was, however, painted white in the wake of the British attack on Washington in 1814 when British troops burnt down all the public buildings, including the Presidential Palace, as it was then called. The building was painted white to mask the smoke stains and has remained white ever since. The interior has continued to be restyled at frequent intervals to suit the taste of each resident. Below: the oval study. Overleaf: The Washington Monument reflected in the marble of the Vietnam Memorial.

expected commercial boom was noticeably failing to take place.

When a friend of John Adams, soon to be the second president, named James Greenleaf offered to buy no less than 3,000 lots at $66.50 each the Commissioners charged with the selling the plots jumped at the offer. Before the deal was finalized, Greenleaf brought in a partner named Morris and changed the proposal. It was now agreed that they should reserve 6,000 lots at $80 each, but that the partners would only pay for them and take possession when they had sold them on to developers. Hoping that Morris and Greenleaf would do a good publicity job and get the

President Adams arrived knowing that he, at least, could count on having a house in which to live. His problem was finding it. He and his wife drove down from Baltimore in a carriage and entered the District of Columbia rather uncertain as to what they would find. They discovered the area to be virtually untouched farmland and forests dotted with the houses of the locals. The grand avenues and streets were marked out by stakes scored with surveyors' symbols. Rather bewildered the Adams couple drove around for more than two hours before they managed to get their bearings and head for the center of the 'city.'

The Adams family remained in Washington only a few months before being replaced by the Jeffersons. With the new President the development of the city began to increase in pace. Jefferson refused to move into the Presidential Palace until it was finished, staying at a boarding house in the meantime. He also abandoned any hope of gaining money from the sale of property to finance public buildings and persuaded Congress to appropriate money for the purpose. He also planted poplars along Pennsylvania Avenue in an attempt to improve the grandeur of the street.

According the plans drawn up by L'Enfant Pennsylvania Avenue was to be the main ceremonial parade route of the new capital. It linked the Capitol with the Presidential Palace and was destined to be a planned vista as well as the route taken by processions. When Thomas Jefferson planted his trees the avenue was still in a sorry state. The route between the two principal buildings passed across a shallow hollow which, in wet weather, became marshy and damp. The road was often impassable due to the mud. The commissioners tried to build a firm pavement using stone chips produced by the masons dressing stones for the Capitol. It was a failure for the chips were so sharp they

JERRY W PEOPLES · PHILIP D MONSON · GREGORY S MORGAN
...THY Jr · CLIFFORD E BENCH · DAVID M SEXTON · MICHAEL H RICHARDS ·
...E RATAJCZAK · EDMUND E ROBERGE · RAYMOND J SAATHOFF · GARY J FUQUA · JAMES L GETTER
...AUMAN · LEWIS A DAVIS · MICHAEL J S DEPAUL · CRAIG M DIX
...HARRY C KING · LAWRENCE E LILLY · WILLIAM G NEWBOULD
...ER BOBBY G HARRIS · DOUGLAS M SEELEY · BRYAN J SUTTON
...NS · ALAN B BOFFMAN · KEITH A BRANDT · JOHN R CHAMPLIN
...CK L CRISTMAN · RICARDO MARTINEZ GARCIA · JON M SPARKS
...GENE R KENNEDY · THORNTON L WOOLRIDGE · JACK L BARKER
...DENNIS T DARLING · WILLIAM E DILLENDER · JOHN F DUGAN
...HAEL E KOSCHKE · VINCENT C MAURO Jr · ROBERT P MARTIN Jr
...WILLIAM E ROYAL · JAMES D SCHOOLEY · JOHN L TRUESDELL
...DONALD J FRAZELLE · ERNEST L HIRTLER · DAVID C LANCASTER
...RLING · LARRY M MASON · CLAUDIUS A SMALL · ANDRE B TIMS
...ISTOPHER Z CZARNOTA · TERRY W DOAN · KARL W DRUZINSKI
...E · WILLIAM S GLENN · STEPHEN D GUCOFSKI · WALTER R HALL
...DONALD P KNUTSEN · JEROME E LE ROY · LARRY D LEMON
...PETER G MORIARTY · JOHN W McLEMORE Jr · ROGER W STAHL
...VER III · GARY S WHITE · THOMAS L ZEIGLER · SHERMAN AVANT
...RTH · JOHN D HEINZ · DENNIS M HOTALING · JEFFREY C KELLY
...LANCE A ROBINSON · WILLIAM L SCHELL · WARREN P SE...
...CURTIS D BAUER · HARRY M BECKWITH III · DAVID L CO...
...ABEE · JOHN C MERRITT · WILLIAM E ...HERMAN · THOM...
...IAM D SMITH · GREGORY M STONE ...ME M ETHOM...
...AEL D WRIGHT · BERNARDO KE... IOS · EDDIE ·
...WN Jr · MAXIMINO ESTRADA ...OYLE FOSTER · GARY ...
...N Jr · OLIN D MARLAR III · R D McDONELL · JEFFREY M...
...RY A SIMONSON · JEROME E JACKSON · RANDALL A...
...UENTES · JACOB B BABIN Jr · ROBERT O COFFEY · ...
...WILLIAM A KINDER · VINCE R KISELEWSKI · DEAN W KRUEG...
...LIPS · JAMES M RISCH · GARY A SCHULTZ · GORDON E TIBB...
...LD ZLOTORZYNSKI · ROBERT T BRADLEY · ROBERT G CHACE...
...JOHNSON Jr · THOMAS P OLSON · PAUL E SERVEN · GLEN H VE...
...NALD J BECKSTED · DONALD C BENNETT · VICTOR R BENNE...
...D · RICHARD R CARSON · CLIFFORD W CORR · LARRY D AUSTIN
...ON · KYLE S HAMILTON · DRUEY LEE HATFIELD · JOHN L HOGAN
...WILLIAM W KIRKPATRICK · RICHARD V KNIGHT Jr · LARRY P LAND
...McGEE · LARRY W McKEE · LAYMON PALMER · STEVEN D PLATH
...ETT · WARREN P RITSEMA · DALLAS D ROBINSON · PAUL A SHEER
...JOSEPH R RYAN Jr · DONALD M STOTTS · ROGER D WHIRLOW
...ARLES H EDWARDS Jr · KENT D ERICKSON · MICHAEL A FRATTALI
...KIMBER · LESTER J MOE · ROGER A PEDERSON · BARRY A RHASE
...Jr · CRAWFORD H TRAVER · ALLEN E KINSMAN · JAMES H ALLEN
...I · RONALD CLEVELAND · AMADO ALANIZ Jr · DAVID F NIDEVER
...LIFF · ROBERT J SKEWES · MICHAEL A WADE · MICHAEL A YOUNG
...LAZO · ROBERT LEE · RANDOLPH L MARTHE · HAROLD E MYERS
...ARNELL · ROGER G REID · JAMES SALLEY Jr · GUY G SHANNON Jr
...MICHAEL L THOMPKINS · HARRIS L WILLIAMS · JOHN W ANDERS
...DONALD J HAVEL · ARTHUR HERNANDEZ · JAMES A HIGHSMITH
...TER L WINTER · STEVEN C WRAY · GEORGE W YOUNGERMAN Jr
...ES R MEADE · JAMES E SUTHERLAND · JOSEPH M YOUNGERMAN
...D R BLACKSMITH · WAYNE R BOROWSKI · HOWARD J BOWER Jr
...RAYFORD H KING · ROBERT J KISER · KENNETH A THOMASON
...S B LOW · FELIX MARCIAL TRUJILLO · HOWARD O WARBINGTON
...S Sr · MICHAEL E GIESE · BENNY E HART · ROBERT W HOMSCHEK
...NNY H LAWRENCE · HARVEY M REYNOLDS · JOSEPH S SMITH
...ELVIN C WHEELER Jr · JAMES P ALEXANDER · KARL R BERBERT
...ND · GARY J FIEDLER · DAVID B FITZGERALD · ARTHUR GLASS
...MICHAEL M SCOTT · FRANK T BURTON · CLAUDE R GIBBONS
...RD J LOCKWOOD · DONNIE C TAYLOR · LEONARD J TRUMBLAY
...OD · EARL H KING · RICHARD MORGAN · GROVER C PIERSON Jr
...DEATHERAGE · JOHN GLOVER · THOMAS L SONDERMAN
...ALLAN F WILKINS · LEVI J WILSON · MATT J WODARCZYK
...LBUR GREENE · CARROLL B LILLY · NEWELL F APPLEGATE Sr
...OHN H FRANKS · ROBERT L GROF · GREG N HENDERSON
...MARTIN T McDONALD · JACK L KING · STEVEN W MANESS
...RONG · WAYNE C BAGGETT · CLARENCE R FRANKLIN
...EUS DENNIS · JACK P BEGLEY Jr · JEAN P HUMBERT
...ARD P PILKINGTON · JOSEPH A SCHOOLMEESTERS
...DENNIS G DONOVAN · ALFONZO L ESPINOZA Jr
...BENJAMIN J BENAVIDEZ · JAMES A NICHOLS
...WILLIAMS · RENE A ZIMMERLE · TERRY JOE BAILEY
...ALL · JAMES JILES Jr · RONNIE A KERR · THOMAS E MACKEY
...LM NOLEN · ABRAHAM POWELL · RONALD L SANBOWER
...ES · LARRY L BROWN · BRUCE E BUTCHER · JEFFRY E COWLEY
...INGER · TERRY W GREENE · ROBERT C HEIN · PAUL McKENZIE
...RRY S STEARNS · GREGORY A TYNES · WILLIAM J WARD Jr
...ELS · DAVID R DEKKER · LEE E BRIMSLEY · DAVID R KOWITZ
...AUL C SAWTELLE · ULMER J WATSON · BARRY E BROWN
...WILLIS N ANDREWS · MICHAEL E BALL · JAMES R THOMAS
...ARS Jr · GEORGE J ORR · GARY L REYNOLDS · RAYMOND E HAUSER
...ENTER · JOSEPH L COX · RONALD J PETERS · GABRIEL L TWOEAGLE
...QUILES-HERNANDEZ · JOHNNY SAXON · BRUCE D OLSON
...OHN S GENTKOWSKI · KENNETH M HATCHER · DANNY G DRINKARD

Charles Paul Ellis

GEORGE T TAYLOR
GARY A ...
RALPH E...
LARRY R DEW...
MICHAEL D...

...WANN · SCOTT W WYATT · EDWARD A WE... · ...EW C STRONG III
...CHEZ Jr · MICHAEL A LAMUSGA · GEORGE H POTTS · ...KEVIN P FORCUM
...TERRY K BEGGS · RANDALL J BOYD · JOSE ANGEL SA... · ...RD D THOMAS · MICHAEL...
...JAMES W MYLES · REY FRANCISCO TORRES-RAMOS · LEM ... · DANIEL M BROWN
...LARRY LEE MILLER · DAVIS J MORGAN · WILLIAM K TAYER... · BILLY H WYATT · EDMOND
...HAROLD E BARNARD · CARL W BORCHERS · MARTIN E LOVE... · MICHAEL R STREET · BERN...
...S F BAUMGARDNER Jr · DAVID C BROWN · ANTHONY M ... · JERRY L THOMAS · MAURIC...
...THOMAS H FARMER · HIAWATHA H WILLIAMS · JOHN R MICKLE · THOMAS E EPPERSON · STEPHEN...
...MICHAEL M DALTON · HUGH A SEXTON Jr · ROBERT L SIMMONS · JOHNNY ARTHUR · CARL ...
...LOUIE G MONTOYA · WILLIAM C BILY · THOMAS J CONNER... · JOHNNY JACKSON · LOYD...
...THOMAS ... BEATTY · CARROLL J BENTON · RALPH L CHURCH · GARY J PFLASTER
...RICHA... · JOSEPH D HAYES · JAMES D JACKSON · CHARLES A SANCHEZ · GARY ...
...LEONARD L BRO... · FRANKLIN T CRITES · DENNIS M DICKE... · ...REY D SCHUMACHER · EAR...
...MAN ... · ANTHONY A PRICE · WAYNE A C... · WILLIAM T WALSH
...LOYD L BRADSHAW · ...LVESTER C MARTINEZ · BILLY D PEDING... · JAMES A SOUTHER · RICHARD...
...DONALD WOOD · THOMAS R HARVEY · DANNY G S... ARD · ERNEST K TYLER
...WAYNE J BRILLEAUD · DAVID L CURTIS · ERNEST ... · HAROLD E IMLER Jr
...HILIP LEE · VINCENT ... · BARRY A BIDWELL... · ...ND V DEBLASIO · JOH...
...FOR COOK ... · ...ANDY V HINES · L...
...WILLIAM E REED
...WHEELER D...

For many years the 58,156 Americans killed or missing in the Vietnam War had no national memorial due to the unpopularity of the war and public feeling about the methods employed in fighting it. Eventually veterans' organizations received permission to erect a monument on the Mall. The stark black marble wall listing the name of every citizen killed or lost (above and far left) was designed by Maya Lin and was dedicated in November 1982 at an impressive ceremony (facing page). Two years later a statue of three young soldiers was added (left and overleaf) together with an American flag.

tore boots apart.

The land speculators then went bankrupt, thus releasing new areas of the city for development. Boarding houses and taverns began to emerge on the flanks of Capitol Hill. The grander private houses still tended to be built to the northwest, where Massachusetts and Pennsylvania Avenues entered Georgetown.

In an attempt to quicken the pace of development President Jefferson split the District of Columbia in three in 1802. The City of Washington had jurisdiction over the area originally planned by L'Enfant. The City of George-

town encompassed that already established town while the County of Washington covered the rest. It was hoped that local control by civic authorities would speed things up. Slowly the city began to take shape as increasing numbers of officials moved to Washington, to be followed by newspapermen and the tradesmen who could earn a living serving their wants.

The nation too was growing. Jefferson saw Ohio join the Union as the seventeenth state and made the Louisiana Purchase, which doubled the size of the nation at a stroke. With growth, the responsibilities and power of the Federal

government in Washington increased accordingly. The city grew slowly as more public servants moved into town. The expected commercial boom, however, was still noticeably absent. L'Enfant had confidently included docks and wharves in his plans, but most of them were never needed.

The business of government continued nonetheless and soon one question began to dominate all others; relations with Britain. Friction with the former colonial power was increasing in two main areas, on the western frontier and in the North Atlantic. Under a treaty of 1794 Canadians had been granted certain commercial rights in the western territories claimed by America. The Canadians alleged these rights were being infringed while the Americans believed that the Canadians were inciting trouble among the Indians and causing them to attack American settle-

ments.

The tension was increased by the behavior of the British Royal Navy. Britain had been at war with Napoleonic France for over a decade and the Royal Navy was imposing a policy of 'stop and search' on all neutral ships heading for Europe in case they were carrying war materials to France. The majority of these ships were American merchantmen whose owners were making handsome profits from trading with both France and Britain which had embargoed each other's goods. In Washington a strong warhawk faction grew up which demanded war against Britain. The members made passionate speeches describing 'insults to the flag' perpetrated by the Royal Navy and the atrocities committed by Indians allegedly acting with Canadian support.

On 19th June 1812 the United States, under President Madison, declared war on Britain. The War of 1812, as it became known, was to have a decisive effect on the city of Washington, though at first nothing could have seemed more unlikely. Congressman Henry Clay declared to Congress that 'the militia of Kentucky alone are competent to place Montreal and Upper Canada at your feet.'

As soon as the winter snows melted the American invasion of Canada began. In April a fleet of American warships landed a strong force at York, now Toronto, the capital of Upper Canada, now Ontario. In the bitter fighting both sides suffered casualties and the British were forced to burn their largest warship on the Great Lakes to prevent its capture. The American troops took possession of the city, looted it and burnt the government buildings to the ground.

When he heard the news the flamboyant and boastful British Admiral Sir George Cockburn sent a message to President Madison saying that he would soon be coming to 'make his bow' at the Presidential Palace in Washington. Nobody took Cockburn's threat seriously for the British were on the defensive in Canada, and were heavily involved in the European war. By the close of 1813, however, the American invasion of Canada had ground to a halt and the Royal Navy had established its dominance in the North Atlantic.

On 23rd August 1814 a messenger galloped into Washington with the news that Admiral Cockburn had

sailed his fleet into Chesapeake Bay and was putting ashore a force of troops under General Ross. Nobody had any doubts that Cockburn had come to carry out his promise made over a year earlier. The local militia was hastily called out and concentrated at Bladenburg to block the road to Washington. Early on 24th the militia was defeated and the British marched for the capital.

President Madison gathered together the papers of state and carried them off to Lewisburg, 35 miles to the north. As the day wore on, most of the citizens followed the lead of their President and fled to the interior. One of the few to stay on was Dolley Madison, the First Lady. She expected

and ordered his men to take the seats of Congressmen. With an ironic, and cruel sense of humor, the officer then put forward the motion 'Shall this harbor of Yankee Democracy be burned?'. It was passed unanimously. The officer ordered his men to pile furniture and barrels in the center of the building, and then set it alight. Before long smoke was curling out of the South Wing of the Capitol as the fire took hold. Minutes later flames licked hungrily from the North Wing.

Pushing on to the Presidential Palace, the jubilant British found the meal Dolley Madison had not had time to eat laid in the dining room of the Presidential Palace. The

Facing page top and below: The Tomb of the Unknown Soldier in Arlington National Cemetery is guarded continuously by an honor guard provided by the 1st Battalion 3rd US Infantry. The guard is changed every hour in winter and half hour in summer with much ceremony. Left: The eternal flame which burns on the tomb of President John F. Kennedy in Arlington National Cemetery. Only one other President is buried in Arlington, William Taft who held office between 1909 and 1913 and went on to become Chief Justice in 1921. Facing page bottom: The grounds of Arlington.

her husband to return, and in the meantime was determined to save as much as possible from the vengeful Cockburn and worked frantically to send valuable objects away. Looking around for signs of approaching aid, Dolley Madison could see 'only groups of military wandering in all directions as if there were a lack of arms or of spirit to fight for their own firesides.' In truth the local militia was disorganized and dispirited by their recent defeats.

At three o'clock Dolley Madison packed as much as possible into a wagon and sent it off towards the west though as she noted in her diary 'Whether it will reach its destination - the Bank of Maryland - or fall into the hands of British soldiery, events must determine.'

In the late afternoon, as she and her servants struggled to unscrew the magnificent portrait of Washington by Gilbert Stuart from the wall, Daniel Carroll arrived to tell her that the British scouts were within sight and the militia were falling back through the city. A servant produced a knife and cut the precious portrait from the frame. Dolley Madison grabbed the picture and fled with Carroll. She spent the night in a militia tent, the painting safe in her possession.

The British troops arrived soon after Dolley Madison had fled. As General Ross approached the first large building, the home of Mr Sewall, a drunken Irish barber leapt out of hiding to fire his musket at the approaching officer. The shot missed Ross, but struck his bay mare squarely in the heart and killed her instantly. Ross was pitched forwards into the dust, which did little to endear the city to him. The barber ran off before the British could catch him.

A British officer led a troop of his soldiers into the Capitol. Finding the House of Representatives empty of its usual incumbents, the officer leapt into the Speaker's Chair

soldiers ate the food gratefully, then put the torch to the building and watched it burn. General Ross led his troops through the city of Washington, methodically laying waste all government property and burning public buildings, together with the naval stores and small wharves on the Potomac. As the British soldiers prepared their evening meal they watched Washington burn.

The fortunes of both Washington and the nation of which it was capital were at their lowest point since both had come into being. But even as the flames licked around the walls of the Capitol, the city's luck was changing.

Storm clouds gathered over the city, drenching the

Below: A view across the ceremonial sights of central Washington at night, showing the floodlit Lincoln Memorial, Washington Monument and the Capitol. Right: The Kennedy Center for the Performing Arts which was opened in 1971 as the home of the National Symphony Orchestra and as the site of five theaters. The centre was granted funds during President Kennedy's administration and has been named as an artistic monument to him. Facing page: The Mall from the Capitol.

British and dousing the raging fires. Early next morning the British pulled out. General Ross believed that the Americans had large forces in the area which would soon concentrate against him. The troops were loaded back aboard the ships of Admiral Cockburn, who sailed off to receive promotion and a coveted colonial governorship. He eventually rose to be First Lord of the Admiralty, the highest position in the Royal Navy.

As the British rearguard left the city, the residents returned to find all the public buildings, except the Patent Office, smoking ruins, but the private buildings untouched. Congress hastily met in Blodgett's Hotel to continue the business of running the nation, and the war. A vote was held as to whether or not the government should stay in Washington. The military vulnerability of the site had been demonstrated in dramatic fashion and many

congressmen pressed for the capital to be moved to a more secure inland site.

Many private citizens were of the same opinion. One highly influential resident wrote to a friend that 'I do not suppose the Government will ever return to Washington.' There was great concern among Washington residents that the money they had invested in houses and hotels would go to waste if the capital was moved elsewhere. In the final vote Congress decided by a majority of just nine to stay in Washington.

Thomas Jefferson summed up the feelings of most Americans when, a few weeks later he wrote to the Marquis of Lafayette that the pillage of Washington had had the effect of 'marking to the world of Europe the vandalism and brutal character of the English Government. It has merely served to immortalize their infamy.'

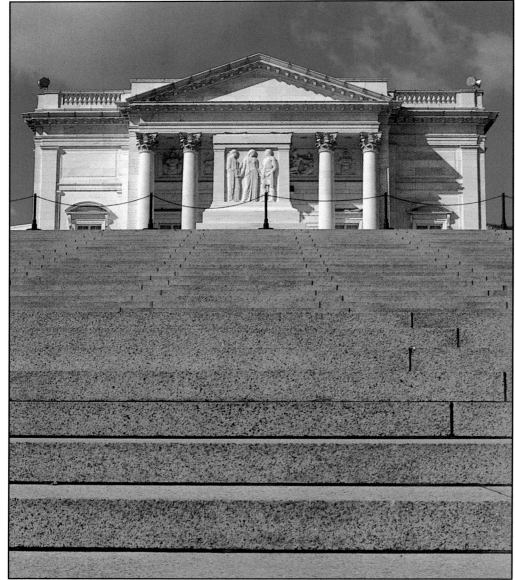

temporary home at Octagon House.

The task of rebuilding the capital got under way as soon as peace returned. A brick building for the Congress was erected from donations by citizens of the city on the site of the present Supreme Court. The Presidential Palace had been gutted by fire, but the sandstone walls still stood. These were given a coat of white paint to hide the scorch marks left by the British and the interior was fully rebuilt. The total cost was $15,567.43, including the price of reframing the portrait of Washington and the purchase of French-style furniture. It was finished by 1817 in time for President Monroe to take up residence. Two years later Congress was able to move out of its temporary brick building and back into the Capitol. The nation's capital was back in business as a government center.

Monroe, who oversaw much of the reconstruction of Washington as a capital city, had an impeccably American background. His great great grandfather had settled in Maryland as early as 1641, though the family later moved to Virginia. As a young man he had fought bravely during the Revolutionary War, being wounded and finishing as a major. Like all the previous Presidents, Monroe was a gentleman farmer from Virginia who had been brought up on the solid virtues of his class. He always dressed well, if not in the peak of fashion and seems to have been devoted to the nation. It was, for instance, during his Presidency that the Stars and Stripes was officially adopted as the national flag of the United States.

The self confidence of the city increased when news of General Andrew Jackson's victory over the British at New Orleans was received in January 1815. Jackson had defeated a force of 5,000 British regulars with only 3,000 men at his disposal and at a cost of just 20 casualties. The peace treaty signed at Ghent was even more welcome for it confirmed an advantageous western boundary between Canada and the United States. The morale of Washington society was boosted further by the vivacious Dolley Madison who tirelessly organized balls and parties in her

SWORN UPO
WE HOLD THESE TRUTHS TO BE SELF-EVIDENT: THAT ALL MEN ARE CREATED EQUAL, THAT THEY ARE ENDOWED BY THEIR CREATOR WITH CERTAIN INALIENABLE RIGHTS, AMONG THESE ARE LIFE, LIBERTY AND THE PURSUIT OF HAPPINESS, THAT TO SECURE THESE RIGHTS GOVERNMENTS ARE INSTITUTED AMONG MEN. WE··· SOLEMNLY PUBLISH AND DECLARE, THAT THESE COLONIES ARE AND OF RIGHT OUGHT TO BE FREE AND INDEPENDENT STATES···AND FOR THE SUPPORT OF THIS DECLARATION, WITH A FIRM RELIANCE ON THE PROTECTION OF DIVINE PROVIDENCE, WE MUTUALLY PLEDGE OUR LIVES, OUR FORTUNES AND OUR SACRED HONOUR.
THOMAS JEFFERSON

Facing page: The statue of Thomas Jefferson which stands 19 feet tall and was crafted by Rudolf Evans. The interior walls of the monument are engraved with excerpts taken from the two documents of which Jefferson was himself most proud. The first was the historic Declaration of Independence and the second was the Statute of Religious Freedom drafted for the Virginia Assembly. Although less well known than the Declaration, the Statute encapsulated much of Thomas Jefferson's thoughts and beliefs. Left: The exterior of the Jefferson Monument showing the impressive silhouette of the statue.

The design of the flag was derived from the armorial bearings of the Washington family. These consisted of three white stars on a blue bar set over horizontal red and white stripes. The motifs were adapted to their new role by increasing the number of stars to match the number of states, and doing the same for the stripes. The origin of such a development might be traced back to the old medieval practice of creating battle flags. Under this system each knight and lord had a personal banner which carried his arms or some schematic derivation of them. This was used as a rallying point by the troops of that man. Washington's use of a stylized version of his coat of arms as a battle flag simply continued the tradition.

It was under the eye of Monroe's First Lady, Elizabeth

Monroe, that the interior furnishings of the new White House were largely put together. The costly French-style furnishings were magnificent, but attracted some criticism on the grounds of extravagance. The redecoration was nearly completed when, on 9th March 1820, Washington saw one of many firsts. Monroe's daughter Maria was married in the White House, her marriage becoming the first within a Presidential family to take place in the capital.

Monroe's administration also saw an improvement in the image of the capital city itself. L'Enfant's plans for boulevards and avenues had never fully been realized. Many of the intended thoroughfares remained little more than staked out pathways. Some avenues lacked any sign of existence at all. In 1820 it was decreed that the more rural activities of the region would have to take definite second place to the business of government. Farmers were banned from planting crops beside the roads, and they were forbidden to leave tools or equipment on public thoroughfares. The effects of these measures was to clean up the streets so that they began to resemble the elegant routes which L'Enfant had intended them to be. At the same time the rustic feel to the city was removed, and with it the target of a large number of ribald remarks from the citizens of more established cities, such as New York and Phi-

Thomas Jefferson, whose impressive memorial was completed in 1943 was probably the most intelligent and best educated man ever to hold the office of President of the United States. Not only was he one of the authors of the Declaration of Independence, but also devised the monetary system of dollars and cents, negotiated treaties with European powers and served as Governor of Virginia, Secretary of State and President. It is sad to relate that his great abilities could not save him from bankruptcy as an old man.

ladelphia.

The Capitol too was changing. Latrobe was recalled to Washington from Pittsburgh, where he had been designing revolutionary steamboats, to restore the Capitol. He found that 'parts of the walls, arches and columns of the late buildings are in a state requiring a small expense for workmanship and materials, to preserve them from injury from the weather and from falling down.'

Latrobe therefore set about restoring the gaunt shells to their previous condition. He brought in massive pillars, each carved from a single block of marble for decoration and did his best to recreate the old buildings as they had been before the British came. He wrote, soon after work began, that 'All the new work is so constructed as in no part whatever to bear on the old walls, but to serve as a support to them; and the whole is so bound and connected together as to render the building much more strong and durable than it was before the conflagration.' Four years later the arch over the entrance to the Senate Chamber fell down. It was hurriedly repaired.

In November 1817 Latrobe retired to attend to personal matters. He left behind him plans for the completion of the central block of the Capitol to link the two wings. These were based, in part, on Thornton's original design but had been much altered by Latrobe. The new architect, Charles Bulfinch of Boston, was handed the plans and asked to complete the building. But Bulfinch was no happier with Latrobe's plans than Latrobe had been with Thorntons and he made many changes.

Within a year the foundations of the central block were laid, but thereafter work proceeded slowly. This was largely due to changes of plan which continued to take place. At one time it was even suggested that the dome be abandoned together with the rotunda beneath it. Fortunately this change of plan was not implemented, the size and shape of the dome merely being altered instead. The finished dome was of copper-covered wood and rose high above the lower domes over the wings.

The central block was finally completed in May 1828, whereupon Bulfinch left Washington to return to New England. Its cost was put at $1,108,904.43 by the Treasury, which had paid the bills. With the final touches to the central block it appeared that the Capitol was finally finished. The plans of Thornton were complete, although in much altered form, and the Capitol finally appeared as it was intended to do when first begun 35 years earlier. But time was to show that a larger Capitol still was to be needed as the nation itself grew larger.

Included in the brief for the Central Block was an instruction for a crypt. Bulfinch dutifully built such a room beneath the rotunda, creating a magnificent ceremonial resting place, but it was destined never to be used for its original purpose. It was intended by Congress that the remains of George Washington should lie in the crypt. It was felt appropriate that the father of the nation should rest

beneath its Capitol. But permission was needed from the Washington family for such a move.

J.C. Calhoun, President of the Senate, and A. Stevenson, Speaker of the House of Representatives therefore wrote to John Washington, nephew of the President, in order 'to make application to you for his remains, to be removed and deposited in the Capitol at Washington, in conformity with the resolution of Congress.' But they received a brusque response.

'Gentlemen,' wrote John Washington, 'I have received with profound sensibility this expression of the desire of Congress, representing the whole nation, to have the custody and care of the remains of my revered relative; and the struggle which it has produced in my mind between a sense of duty to the highest authorities of my Country and private feelings, has been greatly embarrassing. But when I recollect that his will, in respect to the disposition of his remains has been carried into full effect and that they now repose in perfect tranquility surrounded by those of other endeared members of the family, I hope Congress will do

At a dinner to honor a number of Nobel Prize winners in 1962, President John F. Kennedy joked that it was 'the most extraordinary collection of talent, of human knowledge, that has ever been gathered together at the White House, with the possible exception of when Thomas Jefferson dined alone.' Jefferson was, indeed, a remarkable man being skilled in politics, trade, architecture, art and business. There can be no doubt that his contribution to the nation fully deserves the Jefferson Memorial (these pages) which honors his memory.

Below: The Francis Scott Key Bridge which crosses the Potomac at Georgetown with the great monuments of the Mall beyond. Right: A view of the Washington Monument reflected the in the Reflecting Pool of West Potomac Park. Far right and facing page: The Washington Monument surrounded by cherry blossom. The original design called for not only the towering Egyptian-style obelisk but also a Greek temple-style building at the base thus mixing motifs from two ancient civilizations.

was perfectly healthy and there was no reason why he should not produce a large family and so deprive the United States of the money, and their institution. The workings of fate which were to bring the Smithsonian Legacy to Washington and would create the Smithsonian Institution lay far in the future.

Meanwhile, Jackson had other matters to occupy his time. The most pressing was to arrange his inauguration, at a time when he was still grieving the death of his wife three months earlier. Nonetheless the procession along Pennsylvania Avenue from the White House to the newly

completed Capitol was an impressive affair with numerous carriages and horsemen and Jackson being accompanied by numerous gentlemen and farmers.

Jackson was the last President to be able to enjoy a direct ride from the White House to his inauguration. Today the Treasury Department Buildings stands in the way, necessitating an awkward diversion for the procession. And it was Jackson who was responsible for the construction of the building. By the time Jackson took office it was clear that the growing dominance of Federal government over that of the states meant that government departments needed far

Right and facing page: The Washington Monument. When it was first suggested that a monument to the first President be erected on this site not only was George Washington still alive, but the Potomac washed against the spot. It was decided to erect a dignified equestrian statue on the banks of the river, but nothing was done to put the plans into effect. By the time the present obelisk had been completed in 1885 the land to the west had been drained so that the site stood surrounded by land, not water. Nonetheless a reflecting pool was installed between the Monument and the Lincoln Memorial so that a suitably pleasing reflection can be gained.

facade of pilasters and columns and its impressive portico approached by a long flight of steps. Beneath the grand structure were built immensely strong vaults to contain the gold reserves of the national government. More than a hundred years after the construction of the building, the vaults served a purpose which its builders could never have imagined. They were fitted out as an emergency shelter for President Roosevelt in case of attack by the Germans. It was feared that naval bombardment by ships such as the *Tirpitz* or *Prinz Eugen*, both large surface raiders, might blast the city. However no such attack occurred and Washington escaped a repeat of the fate of 1814.

The impulsive stick-throwing of President Jackson was typical of the man. Unlike all earlier Presidents, Jackson was not an influential landowner with highbrow tastes. Indeed he was very much a man of the people and the first of the 'log cabin Presidents.' He was the third son of an Irish immigrant, who died before he was born. His widowed mother brought up the three boys, though she could not afford a proper education for them. The Revolutionary War claimed the lives of both his elder brothers, and Jackson himself was captured by the British.

This tough upbringing made Jackson self-reliant almost to the point of extremity. When he knew he was right Jackson would brook no interference and his single mindedness was often thought of as being high-handed and autocratic by those who worked with him. But at least

Right and overleaf: The Capitol was erected in several phases between 1792 and 1961. Several rooms have changed their use over the years. What is now Statuary Hall (facing page top) was once the Chamber of the House of Congress. After Congress moved in 1857 each state was invited to send two statues of famous citizens to decorate the chamber. Several statues, including that of Martin Luther King (above right), are now placed elsewhere in the Capitol. Above: The interior of the rotunda. Facing page bottom: An unknown victim of the Vietnam War lies in state in the Rotunda before being taken to Arlington for a full military burial.

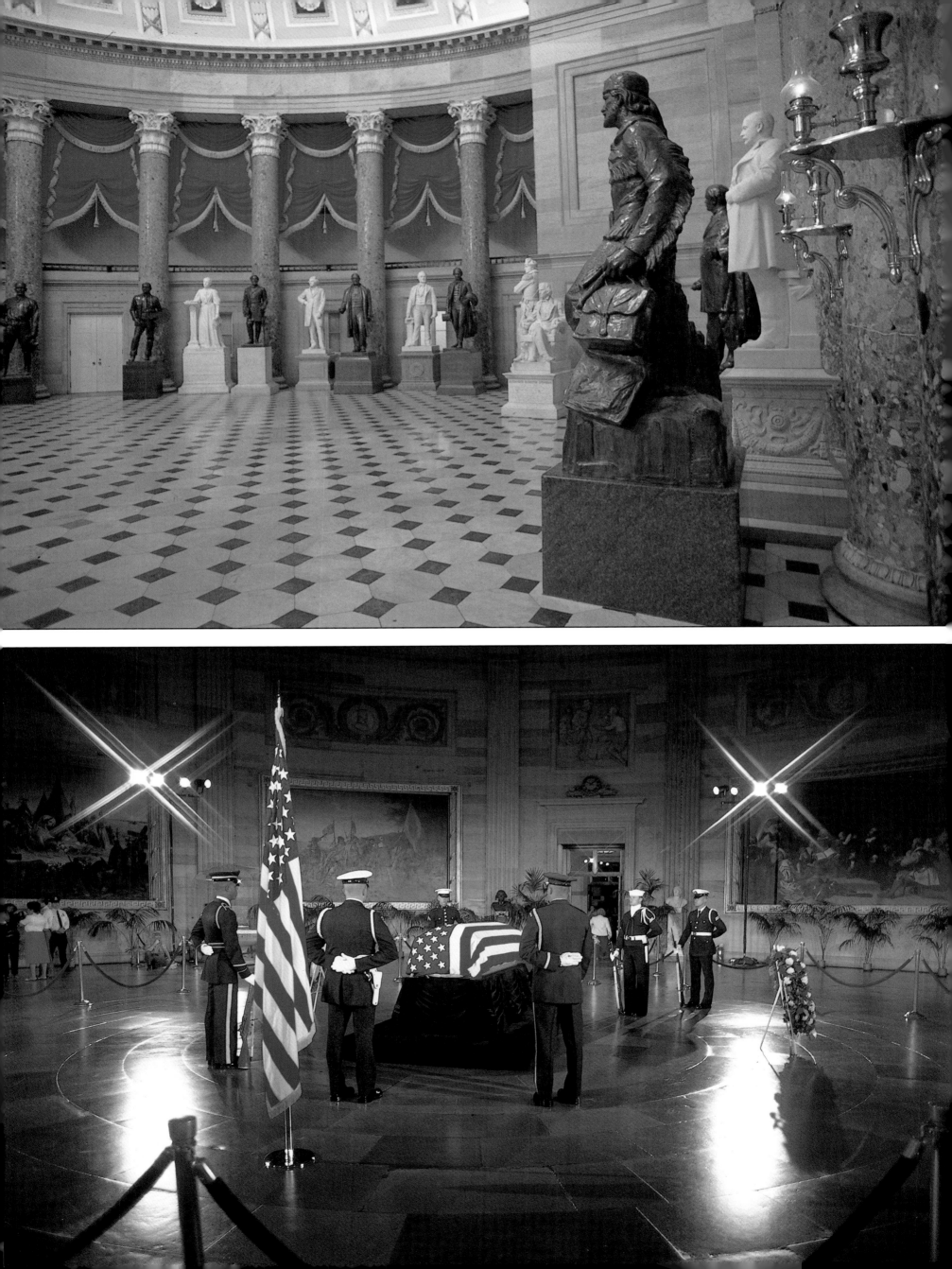

Jackson got things done.

One project which eluded even Jackson's gifts to get it functioning had been begun the year before he took office. This was the Chesapeake and Ohio Canal which was intended to turn into reality L'Enfant's plans for docks and jetties along the Potomac. By pushing a canal inland from the Potomac to the Ohio it was intended to create a southern version of the Erie Canal, already a highly profitable trade route. Gangs of workmen moved in to the

business away from the canal, which suffered accordingly. Once again the economic boom failed to materialize. The city fathers almost gave up all hope of industrialization and Washington is still devoid of commercial enterprises. Nearly everyone in the city is dependent on government employment, organizations hoping to influence government, or on businesses which serve these people.

Another Washington project which seemed set for great things, only to fall into inactivity was the concept of a

Right: A surprisingly rural view of the Capitol dome. This is the second dome to top the Capitol building. The first was erected in the 1820s by Charles Bulfinch of Boston, but this was judged to have been out of proportion when new wings were added in the 1850s and the present cast iron dome was begun to replace it. Below: A hot summer day brings out office workers to rest around the Washington Monument at lunchtime. Facing page: The view of the Capitol from the top of the Washington Monument.

city as work began, gouging out the course of the canal as it snaked westward from Georgetown towards its distant target. Hopes were high that at long last the commercial prosperity which had been predicted for Washington would at last arrive.

The citizens of Alexandria hoped to benefit enormously and persuaded the government to return their town to Virginia. No doubt they hoped to gain a better deal from the state rather than the national administration. In the event, they need not have bothered. The Chesapeake and Ohio Canal was completed only after enormous cost and considerable delays. By the time the last section was dug, the B&O Railroad was also in operation, covering much the same route. The more efficient railroad soon took

magnificent monument to George Washington. L'Enfant had provided a site for just such a memorial in his original plans. He felt it should stand at the heart of the city, on the banks of the Potomac River. When L'Enfant laid his plans the Potomac was both wider and marshier than it is today. The site placed the monument at the crossing point of a north-south axis from the White House and a west-east axis running down from Capitol Hill.

Though the idea of a monument had been included in the original plans, nothing had been done about erecting one. In 1833, however, a National Monument Society was founded with the intention of collecting money and choosing a design. Both activities got off to good starts, with money flowing in and Robert Mills, architect of the Treasury Department, submitting an impressive and imposing design. Mills envisaged a sweeping circular colonnade in the Greek style from which emerged a massive obelisk based on ancient Egyptian models.

The plans were drawn on an epic scale and, from the first, demanded ambitiously large amounts of cash to put them into effect. Work began in 1848 when the cornerstone was laid. Because the plans called for such an enormously heavy monument, the site had to be shifted a short distance to the east where the ground was rather firmer than on the marshy riverbanks. The costs of construction soon began to outstrip the collection of funds, so the planned colonnade was quietly abandoned and work concentrated on the obelisk. Even there financial problems slowed down construction.

The final straw came when a block of stone donated by Pope Pius IX was stolen. Catholics rounded on the anti-papists accusing them of the crime, while the anti-papists pointed out that it was hardly suitable to have a stone donated by one whom they considered to be one of Europe's most autocratic tyrants built into a monument to liberty. In the increasingly bitter recriminations which

followed the question of fund-raising slipped into the background. In 1855 construction work stopped altogether. There was no more money.

As the Washington Monument was staggering towards semi-completion the city was likewise growing in fits and starts. In 1822 the city had counted a population of just 15,000 people. The intended streets of grand town houses remained empty and bordered by fields. Woods crowded in on the public buildings, giving the city a frontier flavor found nowhere else on the Eastern Seaboard.

Visitors from Europe were amazed by what they found. They were used to national capitals being centers of commerce and industry, bustling with hundreds of thousands of people. In Washington they found a city built for government and lacking any signs of prosperity. The grand public buildings were impressive enough for the White House was completed and the Treasury Department and Capitol were nearly so, but the rest of the city seemed lacking. Some Europeans were scathing. The British novelist Charles Dickens wrote of 'public buildings that need but a public to be complete and ornaments of great thoroughfares which need only great thoroughfares to ornament.'

Others were more constructive, such as the bequest of

Facing page top: The Vice-President's House, an Italianate mansion which stands in the grounds of the U.S. Naval Observatory. Facing page bottom: Some of the hundreds of pleasure craft kept by Washington citizens on the Potomac. Above: The British Embassy, designed by the famous British architect Sir Edward Lutyens in 1930, nestled in its finely kept gardens. Left: The tranquil water gardens of the Japanese Embassy. Overleaf: The Washington Monument.

Smithson, whose nephew suddenly died in 1835. As the nephew left no children the entire fortune of around $500,000 passed to the United States Government for the purpose of establishing a scientific body which, in Smithson's own words was 'for the increase and diffusion of knowledge among men.'

Although the money was available, it was not until 1846 that the Smithsonian Institution actually came into being. Even then three years passed before the foundation stone was laid, and a further nine before the Institution was opened. The site chosen was an impressive one in the heart of the Mall, the broad sweep of turf running down from the Capitol towards the then unfinished Washington Monument. The building jutted out into the area earmarked by L'Enfant for gardens and fountains, disrupting the original plan just as the Treasury Department Building had already done.

The building was conceived in the then very latest and most modern style. It was to take the form of a castellated mansion with architectural details reminiscent of Norman England, eight centuries earlier. Many feel that the red sandstone edifice jars against the cool, elegant lines of the Classical style which dominates other major public buildings. It rapidly became a famous landmark, and remains so to this day. The Smithsonian now fills 13 museums, one of which is in New York, and contains some 80 million artifacts. But it is the original 'Castle on the Mall' which symbolizes the whole complex.

By the time the Institution was opened the population of Washington had reached 51,000 as the business of Federal Government became ever more powerful and demanded greater resources of manpower. In 1850 a law was passed

Possibly the most imposing structure in the city is the Washington Monument which dominates many views. The pointed cap was made of aluminum as this was considered more durable than the marble used for the rest of the obelisk. The business of placing the 3,300 pound capstone called for all the ingenuity of the late 19th century. The feat was finally accomplished with the aid of a complex system of self-supporting scaffolding in 1884. The small aluminum peak was then added, bringing the total height up to 555 feet and 5 inches.

permitting slave-owning, but not slave-trading, within the city. Many southerners previously reluctant to move into Washington now entered the city and it soon counted 75,000 inhabitants.

They continued to live in a city which was far less imposing than it had been intended to be over half a century earlier. Most of the streets and avenues had not been built along, let alone surfaced. One disappointed visitor declared that 'taking a map with him in his journeyings a man may lose himself in the streets, not as one loses oneself in London, but as one does so in the deserts of the Holy Land.' Following supposed roads visitors could find themselves sinking up to their knees in bogs or having to scramble over hedges. So wild was the country that the Englishman Anthony Trollope declared he could 'shoot snipe within sight of the President's house.'

The most important thoroughfare of the city was intended to be Pennsylvania Avenue. This road was paved with cobbles and flanked by a brick pavement, but the cobbles were continually needing repair due to poor drainage and were broken in many places by potholes and patches of mud. Geese for sale were driven along the Pennsylvania Avenue and neighboring streets, accompanied by fish sellers and other street traders who filled the air with their raucous cries. Hogs ran free through the central region and tended to congregate around a particularly favorite muddy wallow a few yards from the Capitol.

Pennsylvania Avenue was intended from the start to be the grandest thoroughfare of the city, a status it has achieved with impressive style. Not only does it provide the route taken by official parades, but its sides are the sites of numerous important offices, formal structures, monuments and hotels. Left: Willard Hotel is the second of that name to stand on the site. The first was built in 1850 by Henry Willard and at once became a favorite haunt of politicians, civil servants and army officers. In 1901 the present structure was completed as the last word in luxury and opulence. A complete renovation in the early 1980s has ensured that Willard Hotel remains one of the finest in Washington.

The magnificent public buildings were more impressive, but they were separated by open fields rather than connected by long avenues, and were largely unfinished. The Treasury Department, Patent Office and Post Office were likewise slow in construction, the two former remaining incomplete as late as 1860. The Washington Monument looked forlorn as a bare stump.

Even those structures which had been completed were the subject of some criticism. The White House was viewed by many Europeans and southern plantation owners as a small and rather unremarkable country house. The two equestrian statues by Clark Mills, one of President Jackson and another of President Washington, were considered stilted and poor by the more cultured citizens.

If the Federal government was aiming at great splendor, the district government which actually ran the city seemed content with far less. Local government was administered from a collection of unimpressive offices surrounded by boarding houses and small shops. Though responsible for policing the city, the district government did little in this direction. Only 50 men were on duty at any one time, and most of these were employed in policing the public buildings. Appointments in the police force were treated as rewards for political help during elections with the result

that professionalism barely existed at all. The gangs of 'undesirables' which roamed the streets at night were notorious and most respectable people either traveled by carriage or in groups once night had fallen.

But despite this picture of untidiness and danger, the business of government was booming and taking shape. This activity could best be seen, not in the buildings of state, but in the hotels of Pennsylvania Avenue where, it was rumored, more government business was conducted than at the Capitol. The great public rooms of Willards or the National were thronged almost constantly with congressmen, their secretaries and lobbyists.

Breakfast, dinner, tea and supper became ritualized meetings with some congressmen holding open discussion with passersby, while others indulged in secret and intimate conversations. The meals at the hotels became famous for their opulence, extravagance and political importance. Steak, paté and oysters were regularly on the breakfast menu and richer dishes were commonplace in the evenings.

The Capitol, which everyone had considered to be finished in 1828 was now proving itself to be too small for its purpose. The growing number of states increased the number of Congressmen accordingly while the growing complexities of government led to an increased demand for office space and storage by the Congressmen who already sat. The need for added accomodation was noted as early as

1843 when the Senate asked for plans to be submitted for an extension. The plans arrived, but nothing much was done about them.

The rebuilding work really got under way in 1850. This time, as earlier, there were to be bitter wrangles and acrimonious disputes between architects and patrons before the building finally took shape. In April 1850 Senator Jefferson Davis wrote to the architect Robert Mills asking him to prepare outline plans for two large new extensions to the Capitol, one to the north and one to the south. Mills handed in his plans and estimates on 1st May. The Committee on Public Buildings welcomed the proposals and on 19th September passed a bill which appropriated

$100,000 for construction costs and gave the President the right to choose both designs and architect. Before the project was finished the cost would become $8,075,299.04.

The President at the time was Millard Fillmore, who had a reputation for being rather a nice man, but without any great convictions or personal views. He had come to office as Vice President, stepping into the White House after the death of President Zachary Taylor in 1850. Fillmore does not seem to have been over interested in the project to enlarge the Capitol. He allowed himself to be persuaded by senators who did not care for either Jefferson or Mills and announced a public competition for plans. Once again the

original architect chosen to work on the Capitol was spurned.

The competition was won by Thomas U. Walter of Philadelphia and he was appointed architect in February 1851. Four months later his final plans were officially approved and work was able to begin. Walter's design called for the construction of two new wings, each of which was to be almost as large as the entire Capitol as it then stood. He intended to continue the Classical styling of the Capitol as originally planned by Thornton, but on a grander scale to suit the more prestigious position the United States occupied in the world. He intended to built in marble of a pure and glittering white. Each wing was to be adorned with one hundred pillars with elaborate Corinthian capitals. In order to match the new wings to the old freestone Capitol, Walter intended to reface the old building with marble. In the event the cheaper alternative of painting it white was adopted.

On 4th July 1851 the corner stone of the new extension was laid amid great ceremony. The great procession echoed that of 1793 in its magnificence and pomp, but there were important differences. The Freemasons were still present, but took a subordinate role in the procession. They came third in the order of march and were lumped together with the Sons of Temperance.

Pride of place at the head of the procession went to a small group of elderly men who had fought against Britain in the Revolutionary War and the War of 1812. They were followed by a grand military procession, after which came the President, Congressmen, officials of the city and the few survivors of those who had attended the ceremony of 1793.

The Freemasons came into their own at the actual ceremonial laying, however. Once President Fillmore had laid the stone, the Grand Master of Freemasons stepped forwards to conduct the appropriate ritual of his order. This involved, among other things, adorning the cornerstone with 'the corn of nourishment, the wine of refreshment and the oil of joy'. What the Sons of Temperance thought about the national capitol being bathed in wine is better imagined than recorded.

There then followed a round of speech-making which became well known for the address given by Daniel Webster, then Secretary of State. Now aged 69 Webster was the greatest orator in America, possibly in the English-speaking world, then living. The text of his speech on this occasion is widely recognized as one of his finest. But on the day Webster did not stick to the speech he had written and which has survived. He frequently put his papers down and spoke on some other related subject for

Above: The West Capitol Plaza in winter. Right: The Capitol dome seen through the ring of flags at the base of the Washington Monument. Far right: A parade of men in Revolutionary War uniforms and drill marches down Constitution Avenue, just one of many parades and ceremonies which Washington attracts as the capital city. Facing page: The Grant Memorial backed by the Capitol. The Grant Memorial is one of the largest in the city, embracing not only the central equestrian statue but also a complex of associated works.

some time, before picking up his prepared text again. One contemporary described these digressions as 'extemporised new thoughts and highly interesting reflections.' Interesting they may have been, but they kept Webster on his feet for over two hours. By the time he was finished most of the crowd had probably had enough of speeches and were looking forward to supper and the grand fireworks display to follow.

The first construction problems came to light within days of the great ceremony. Workmen digging the foundations found that the extreme northwest corner of the site was composed of sandy soil which was too unstable to take the massive weight of marble portico planned for it. Walter told the workmen to dig until they found solid substrata.

At thirty feet down the workmen were still uncovering nothing but soft sand. The sides of the excavations needed shoring up to stop them collapsing down and killing the workmen. If Walter was worried he did not show it. He told the men to continue digging. At forty feet they struck rock and Walter knew work could really get under way.

By the end of the year the foundations were complete and by the close of 1854 the buildings had reached ceiling height, though the glass and iron roofs were not added until 1856. Walter was building on the grand Classical scale which had not been seen since the fall of the Roman Empire. His building echoed the lines and grace of the famous Parthenon in Athens, Greece.

The stone to build the structure came from three sources.

emerged, dominated by great plantation owners who ran their estates with the aid of slaves. Even the humblest farmer owned a slave or two to help with the chores. In the North a more industrial and liberal-minded society had sprung up. The differences between the two were great and would prove irreconcilable. It is possible that a peaceful solution to the diverging views of the two halves of the nation might have been found, but the men who occupied the White House in the years leading up to the outbreak of war were not the ones to do it.

For generations the Federal government had been dominated by southerners, Washington himself had been a Virginian. Such a state of affairs had been congenial to the south, which continued to exercise their rights as indepen-dent states, joined in a voluntary union, to make their own laws concerning slavery. But the North was growing in population and wealth and would soon mount a challenge for control of the Federal Government.

In 1845 a southern landowner by the name of James Polk was elected President. Polk was a conscientious worker who toiled long and hard at the White House. But he was also, by common agreement, the dullest man to occupy office up to that date and achieved little of note. He was succeeded by Zachary Taylor, a bluff Virginian soldier who had gained the nickname of 'Old Rough and Ready' in his campaigns. After heroic actions in the Mexican War of 1846, Taylor was elected President in 1848. In the summer of 1850 he was overcome by heat, suffered a severe attack

Above, right and far right: The brooding statue of Abraham Lincoln which stands within the Lincoln Memorial. The statue is surrounded by walls which commemorate the great achievements of Lincoln's Presidency. Two vast murals represent the freeing of the slaves and the preservation of the Union while the words of the Gettysburg Address and the Second Inaugural Speech are engraved on flanking walls. Facing page: Fireworks burst over the floodlit Mall. Overleaf: The Ellipse lawn in front of the White House.

hoped that his northern background and popularity would help solve the growing crisis. But his well-meaning efforts at compromise came to nothing. His own lack of conviction did little to help him persuade others to follow any particular course of action.

It was during Pierce's term of office that the growing tensions between North and South had their first solid and lasting effect on the capital. Since its inception the new dome on the Capitol was intended to be topped with a statue symbolic of Freedom. The famed sculptor of public

change of status to those who knew them. Several of those who saw the original design were unhappy about the cap. Jefferson Davis, then Secretary of War, wrote to the officials in charge of the project 'As to the cap, I can only say, that if seems to me its history renders it inappropriate to a people who were born free and would not be enslaved.' But perhaps more importantly, Davis was also worried that such an open reference to the emancipation of slaves might anger the southern states and so hasten the already threatening conflict.

Facing page top: Awakening, one of several effective modern sculptures in the city. Facing page bottom: Cavalry, one of the flanking statue groups of the Grant Memorial. The entire group took sculpture Henry Shrady 20 years to complete, but he died before the dedication ceremony could be performed. Left: The statue of Major General the Marquis de Lafayette in Lafayette Park which shows the Marquis asking the French National Assembly to send help to the fledgling United States in the War of Independence. Below left: The statue of Albert Einstein outside the National Academy of Sciences which shows the great scientist in relaxed pose. Below: The US Navy Marine Memorial in Ladybird Johnson Park. Overleaf: The Jefferson Memorial and Tidal Basin at night.

monuments, Thomas Crawford, was given the contract. At the time, 1855, Crawford was in Rome, where he had spent much of his youth studying ancient works of art.

In his work Crawford showed that he was heavily influenced by classical models. His concept of Freedom was a stately matron draped in the star-spangled banner, accompanied by the Imperial Roman eagle and adorned with such symbolic articles as a laurel wreath for victory, the rising sun signifying hope, a circlet of stars indicating a divine origin and the floppy cap which symbolized freedom in ancient Rome. In time various alterations were made to the statue, she was given an olive branch to symbolize peace for example, but the most contentious issue was that of her cap.

In ancient Rome the cap of liberty was worn only by freed slaves, not by men born free. It announced their

Davis suggested that the statue be given a sword and helmet to emphasize the need for armed defense of liberty. He asked, however, that the sword be sheathed and the helmet pushed back to show that the nation was at peace, and would only have recourse to war when absolutely necessary. Changes were accordingly made with the helmet being inspired by Indian war bonnets.

The finished statue stood 20 feet tall and weighed over 15,000 pounds. It was delivered to the Capitol grounds

135

and erected on a pedestal on the lawns to the south of the building. It stood there for some years, awaiting the completion of the dome. There was a time when it seemed that the dome might never be finished, for the Union was heading towards collapse.

In 1857 Pierce was replaced by another New Englander, James Buchanan. Buchanan was more perceptive than Pierce, but less popular. He was himself opposed to slavery, but was willing to concede that the Constitution guaranteed the rights of slave-owners. He also realised that if he pushed his own views the Southern States might take advantage of their other Constitutional rights and secede from the Union. He carried out a skilful balancing act between the pro- and anti-slavers and was able to avoid the final confrontation which seemed to be fast approaching. In 1860, Buchanan declared he would not seek re-election in line with his long-held beliefs that Presidents should only occupy office for one term.

He was replaced by a man viewed with deep suspicions by a large part of the nation, Abraham Lincoln. Lincoln came from a poor Kentucky family which later moved to Illinois. After various early jobs, Lincoln became a lawyer and politician. He was a simple and transparently honest man seemingly ill-equipped for the rough and tumble of political life and intrigue. He did, indeed, suffer many setbacks, but his firm grasp of issues assured him of success. On a national scale he was vociferously committed to two principals; the preservation of the Union and the contain-

Above right, above far right and facing page top: The Washington National Cathedral on which construction began in 1907 and still continues. When completed it will be the sixth largest cathedral in the world and will serve all religions. Right and facing page bottom: The Temple of the Church of Jesus Christ of Latter-Day Saints, often termed the Mormon Temple, which stands just outside Washington in Maryland. The 288 foot tall principal spire is topped by a gilded statue of the angel Moroni which weighs over 2 tons. Far right: The National Shrine of the Immaculate Conception built in a Byzantine style is the largest Roman Catholic church in the United States. The extensive structure contains no fewer than 56 shrines and a 56 bell carillon. Overleaf: Crowds gather around the Washington Monument on 4th July.

White House to give the salute to the President, then marched along Pennsylvania Avenue amid cheering crowds to take up residence in the only building large enough to house them, the Capitol. Soon other militia regiments came pouring in to the city, men from Rhode Island, Massachusetts and New York. Many of the officers brought their wives with them and Washington quickly took on the appearance of a fashionable army camp. Tents sprang up around the city, covering more ground than Washington itself.

Morale in the city soared.

The public were not to know that many of the militia regiments had neither experienced officers nor weapons.

The officers were elected by the men, who not unnaturally usually picked the most popular and easy-going man for the job. Such qualities, however, were unlikely to lead to authority or military skill among the officers. The arsenals which had the duty of keeping weapons had often not restocked since the guns were laid up after the Revolutionary War. When the muskets were distributed they were found to be broken, rusty or simply bust. Word went out to industrialists to gear up for war production, and ambassadors in Europe began buying surplus weapons.

In June a small body of cavalry ran into a group of rebels at Fairfax. A few men were killed and the Unionists returned with a handful of prisoners. It was the city's first

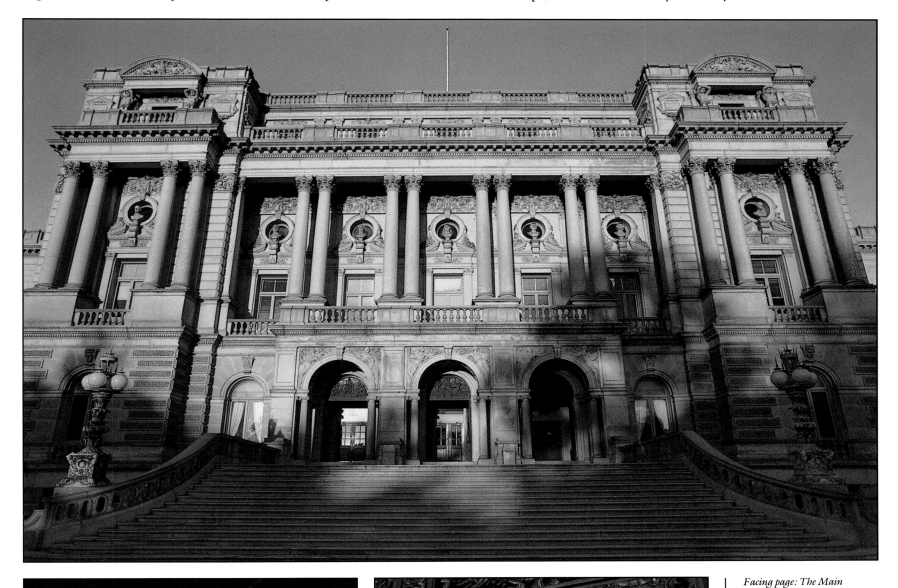

Facing page: The Main Reading Room of the Library of Congress in the Thomas Jefferson Building (above). The ornate building was completed in 1897 but was filled within twenty years and is today augmented by the James Madison Memorial Building and the John Adams Building. The Library of Congress was destroyed in 1814 by the British and was replaced by the private library of Thomas Jefferson. Today the Library of Congress houses around 85 million books, maps, pamphlets and other works. Far left: A statue of James Madison. Left: A plaque on the bronze doors of the Jefferson Building.

147

taste of battle and the citizens eagerly gathered round the newly-blooded troops and gazed at the prisoners. Filled with the flush of victory, the people of Washington began urging the military to advance on Richmond, the new capital of the Confederacy, before the first meeting of the rebel congress on 20th July.

General McDowell was given orders to move out on 9th July to attack the Confederate forces which lay barely thirty miles away. By his own admission McDowell was in command of a collection of troops which were not yet disciplined enough to be called an army. The supply system was rudimentary and McDowell was not certain how long he could stay in the field. Nevertheless, after a week's delay, the Federal army marched out of the capital city. Nearly everyone in Washington was confident that the rebellion would soon be over.

Some, however, hoped otherwise. Although the majority of southerners had left the national capital long before hostilities actually broke out, some remained. The vast majority of shopkeepers and tradesmen in the city had moved in from neighboring areas of Maryland and Virginia. Most of these were doing brisk trade with the soldiers and the officers' families who had temporarily moved into the capital. Whatever their sympathies they were willing to take advantage of the temporary boom in business. Some, however, were determined to do whatever they could to help the Confederate cause. One such was Mrs Rose Greenhow who mixed freely with officers and society ladies. She also ran an efficient message system between Washington and the Confederate General Beaure-

Previous pages: The sun sets behind the flags standing around the base of the Washington Monument. Above right: The impressively business-like Federal Reserve Boardroom in the Treasury Building. Far right and facing page top: The Supreme Court Building was completed in 1935 to house the Supreme Court which had become too large for its old home in the Capitol. Above far right: The judges of the Supreme Court. Facing page bottom: The Library of the Supreme Court. The Supreme Court is responsible for maintaining the integrity of the Constitution and with applying it to new situations and developments as they occur. It decides on less than 200 rulings each year, although some 5,000 are presented. The Supreme Court can even reverse decisions of Congress if it decides that they are unconstitutional. Overleaf: The Castle of the Smithsonian Institution.

way in which a new army, no matter how experienced its officers, could advance after sustaining such losses and Washington was saved. But the atmosphere of the capital had changed. No longer was a quick victory to be expected, and there was no more talk of whipping the rebels before autumn.

The capital city was clearly of enormous importance to the Union. If the Confederate forces could capture Washington it would be an immense blow to the prestige of the Union, while so long as Washington held out the Union could believe in itself.

It was chiefly to further this self confidence that Lincoln continued to spend money on the building of the Capitol dome. When war had broken out the dome was scarcely begun. Now work continued at a steady, but slow pace to remind the citizens, and passing soldiers, that the government was confident of victory. In 1863 the dome was finally finished and the statue of freedom, completed some years earlier, raised into position.

More and more troops were poured into Washington and the city became the center for treatment of the wounded. Munitions and supplies were funneled through the capital and the city became the base for military planning. The capital was becoming increasingly important as a strategic position in its own right, as well as a symbolic prize of immense importance. To protect the city, a series

Known affectionately as "The Castle on the Mall", no. 1000 Jefferson Drive, is the original home of the Smithsonian Institution. The red sandstone structure was built in the then fashionable pseudo-Gothic style in 1849 and stands out in general views of the Mall (these pages). At the time it was intended to have housed the entire Smithsonian collection, and indeed was able to do so for many years. Today the Castle acts as an information center for the collection now fills many nearby buildings.

Facing page top: An ornamental gateway erected in Chinatown to celebrate Chinese New Year. Facing page bottom: The Old Pensions Building, now the National Building Museum. Far left: Ford's Theater where President Lincoln was assassinated by John Wilkes Booth in 1865. After the shooting the theater closed, not to reopen until 1968. Left: The luxurious Willard Hotel. Below: The massive edifice of the Pentagon, now nearly 50 years old.

standing to arms in case Meade chose to launch an assault. Meade did not move either for he had lost 23,000 men and was unsure what to do next. That afternoon clouds rolled up and rain began to pour down. Under cover of the rain and growing dark, Lee began to pull back. Unable to break Meade's army, Lee knew he stood no chance of either taking Washington or of cutting the supply lines to the north. He had lost 27,000 men in the three days fighting and knew that his army needed a rest before it could fight a fresh campaign. Lee, therefore, retreated across the Potomac into friendly territory, with Meade hanging on his flanks.

Back in Washington, the rumors and whispers had been circulating at high level ever since Meade had taken command. On the evening of 1st July news was received that the Confederate forces had been located and that

Meade was advancing. The army Meade commanded had not gained a reputation for success. Indeed it had recently been defeated at Chancellorsville, and the people of Washington had little faith in it.

As news of the battle trickled in, the city remained tense and quiet. Many feared that a defeat would lead to the capture of Washington and the sacking of the national capital. Nobody knew if their lives would be safe or if their property would be burnt. As the evening of 3rd July wore on long-planned celebrations of Independence Day began, but without much enthusiasm. Everyone was too anxious to hear news from Gettysburg to be able to enjoy themselves properly. Rumors of a catastrophic defeat circulated alongside stories of overwhelming victory.

Finally, early next morning, the *Evening Star* newspaper announced the news of Meade's victory. The city went wild

169

in a combination of relief, celebration and 4th July partying. The celebrations became even wilder when it was learned that Vicksburg had fallen.

The siege of Vicksburg had begun in November 1862 when General Grant marched his Unionist army down the Mississippi while General Banks marched upstream from New Orleans accompanied by a fleet of armed river boats. Control of the Mississippi was vital for two reasons. So long as the Confederates could block the river, they could stop the farmers and industrialists of the Mid-West exporting their goods to Europe. This put enormous pressure on the western states, and some considered joining the Confederates if it meant the economic strangulation would end. Additionally the Confederates drew much of their manpower and materiel from west of the Mississippi, bringing it across the river at Vicksburg. So long as the

Confederates held Vicksburg there was a chance they could win the war.

The attacks of November were beaten off with ease, and Grant had to retire and replan. During the winter the Federals attempted to bypass Vicksburg by rerouting the Mississippi and by digging canals, but both schemes failed. In March 1863 Grant was forced into committing his men to a full scale siege. A siege is a long, monotonous and bloody business, but Grant, aided by Sherman, conducted it well. An initial attempt at a surprise assault failed with heavy casualties, and Grant settled down to digging trenches and constructing artillery batteries. Through the long weeks of spring his grip around Vicksburg gradually tightened as outlying defenses were captured and occupied.

In May a short truce was agreed so that the bodies of those who had fallen between the lines could be buried and

messages exchanged. Then the fighting began again. Grant and his men made only slow advances and some began to wonder if Vicksburg would hold out so long that the siege would have to be lifted due to the coming winter. But in Vicksburg conditions were bad. Food was running out, and so was ammunition. Eventually, on 2nd July the Confederate commander offered the surrender, if Grant offered suitable conditions. Grant responded by promising to allow the soldiers to return home, so long as they promised not to fight in the war again. The Confederates agreed and Vicksburg fell.

When news that the vital communications center of Vicksburg had been captured reached Washington, the city went wild. A vast crowd assembled around the White House and, led by a military band, sang patriotic songs to President Lincoln. The crowd surged on through the streets, cheering Grant and Sherman through the night. Many thought that the war was as good as over. It was not to be.

General Meade knew that his army had been savagely mauled at Gettysburg, although it had gained the victory. He was unsure of Lee's intentions and was unaware of the full extent of the Confederate casualties. Not wishing to risk snatching defeat from the jaws of victory, Meade advanced slowly, and Lee got his battered army back to home territory in reasonable shape. When it was realized that Meade had been close to complete victory, criticism of his caution was vitriolic. Even Lincoln noted that a 'golden opportunity is gone.' Meade offered to resign, but there was nobody that the government trusted to take his place and he was kept on.

The mood in Washington slipped into depression. The population settled down to the winter of 1863 knowing that much fighting still needed to be done. Some thought that the Confederacy might yet win, and fears of a raid on Washington remained high. The armies retired to winter quarters for the bad weather made any meaningful type of campaigning impossible. They too awaited the spring. It was to be an eventful spring and summer for the city.

In April the troop movements began. Washington was

Above right: The impressive covered atrium of the International Square office complex. Above far right: The magnificently ornate ceiling of Union Station, which has recently been restored with loving care and thousands of dollars worth of gold leaf. Right: The internal plaza of the International Monetary Fund Building which is the venue for art shows. Far right: Offices in central Washington. Facing page top: Union Station. Facing page bottom: The Watergate complex, scene of the break in which led to the scandal which caused the downfall of the Nixon administration.

guns nervously. At 1.30 pm the first Confederate cannon opened fire, its ball thudding into the ramparts of the defenses. Washington was under siege.

But even as the first siege guns went into action, the danger was passing. Later that afternoon a few regiments of the 6th Corps started disembarking from river boats near the unfinished monument to George Washington. Seasoned campaigners, they were rushed up to the threatened front and before long were pushing forward aggressive patrols.

All the following days the cannons thundered just north of the city, and were clearly audible from the Capitol. That afternoon the telegraph wires to New England were cut and nobody ventured to repair them. But more reinforcements were arriving by ship, in response to the urgent summons of three days earlier. It was on Tuesday that President Lincoln rode out to the advance fortifications to

try to gain an idea of what was going on. After speaking to the officers in command, Lincoln climbed up on to the parapet to get a clearer view. All he received was a bellow from an exasperated junior officer 'Get down, you fool.'

That evening, as the sun sank in red splendor, dust clouds were seen moving behind the rebel lines. Next morning scouts found that the enemy had gone. It had after all been little more than a raid in strength which hoped to catch Washington by surprise. When the veterans of the 6th Corps appeared, the Confederate General Early had decided to fall back. But it had been a close call. If Early had lived up to his name by a day or two he might well have taken the Capital.

It was to be almost the city's last taste of war, almost but not quite. When Early pulled back from Washington most realized that victory for the Union was only a matter of time. But it was also known that the Confederates might

try to prolong the war and so break the Union's resolve to continue. Nonetheless, on 7th April 1865, General Lee surrendered his forces at Appomatox and the war ended. The government and most businesses announced a holiday and the streets were thronged with happy crowds celebrating the return of peace.

But only a week later, on 14th April, President Lincoln was shot dead at Ford's Theater on 10th Street. The assassin was John Wilkes Booth, a fanatical Southerner who wished to avenge the defeat of the Confederate cause. It was the last shot of the war.

Through all the long years of warfare the work of building the Capitol continued. Lincoln recognized that the damage to morale of stopping work would have been immense. It would have appeared that the government itself had despaired of the final victory. Whereas to continue with the work showed that it was believed the Capitol had a role to play in the future. The only possible role it could have was that of a meeting place for representatives from all the states. That could only happen if the Union was preserved. The hammer blows coming from Capitol Hill marked the firm belief of Lincoln and his government in ultimate victory.

Construction work was, however, severely cut back. Money was needed for war supplies, not for marble and transport should have been devoted to moving troops, not cast iron. Nevertheless the work went on. The huge marble pillars were erected one after another to form the porticos

of the mighty new wings.

More visible work continued on the dome which slowly climbed to dominate the skyline of the beleaguered capital. The cast iron sections, weighing nearly 9 million pounds in all, were carefully hoisted and fixed into position. The maze of scaffolding and cranes became an accepted part of Capitol Hill. In 1863 the spherical exterior was complete. At noon on 2nd December 1863 the final section of the statue of Liberty was hoisted into place, a flag was waved by the workmen and field guns in the grounds fired a salute. The workmen then moved on to the interior of the dome, finishing construction work at almost the same time as the final pillar was set up on the Senate Wing.

By the close of 1865, when less than a century old, the capital like the nation had passed through its turbulent years to enter adulthood. Both were firmly established on the international scene as creations of permanence and power. No longer could there be any doubt as to whether Washington would survive, nor whether the Union would survive. Both had grown together, inextricably enmeshed for each is the creation of the other. The capital being a forceful and beautiful symbol of the nation as a whole.

These pages: The smart 19th century townhouses of Capitol Hill were built as residences for congressmen and the administrative staff who served them. Today several are still family homes for those who live and work in Washington, but some have been handed over to foreign nations as embassies. Facing page bottom: The Nepalese (left) and Mauritius embassies.

191

Photographers Index

John Aikins 20/21; 22 (3); 23; 30 (*Bottom*); 44; 45 (*Bottom*); 48 (*Top*); 49 (*Bottom*); 64 (*Bottom left and right*); 65 (*Bottom*); 66 (*Bottom*); 67 (*Bottom*); 81 (*Bottom right*); 89; 92 (*Top left*); 93 (*Bottom*); 97; 105 (*Top*); 107 (*Bottom left*); 110 (*Bottom*); 111 (*Bottom*); 122 (*Top*); 123; 131 (*Bottom*); 136/137; 142; 147 (*Bottom right*); 148/149; 156/157; 160 (*Bottom*); 170 (*Bottom right*); 182 (*Top left*); 183 (*Bottom*); 184/185; 187; 188/189.

S. L. Alexander 14 (*Bottom*); 33 (*Top left*); 34/35; 107 (*Top*); 176; 178 (*Top*); 183 (*Top*).

Ping Amranand 52 (*Top*); 94/95; 99 (2); 116; 152/153; 154 (*Top and bottom right*); 170 (*Top*); 174 (*Top right*).

R. M. Anderson 29 (*Bottom*); 88 (*Top left*); 130 (*Top*); 131 (*Top*);139 (*Top*); 150 (*Bottom right*); 155.

Terry Ashe 92 (*Top right*).

Sue Barew 31 (*Bottom*).

Peter Beck 54/55; 57 (*Top*); 87; 107 (*Bottom right*); 144; 161 (*Top*);168 (*Bottom*); 169 (*Top right*); 178 (*Bottom*).

J. K. Boehm 88 (*Bottom right*).

A. Pierce Bounds 25 (*Bottom left*); 88 (*Top right*); 114 (*Top*); 140/141.

Rick Brady 84 (*Top right*); 169 (*Top left*).

R. Brady 61.

Stephan Brown 172/173.

S. R. Brown 38/39; 138 (*Top left*); 171.

Berle Cherney 138 (*Bottom right*); 147 (*Bottom left*); 177 (*Bottom*).

Paul Conklin 50/51; 67 (*Top*); 88 (*Bottom left*); 93 (*Top*); 135 (*Top*); 151 (*Bottom*); 179 (*Bottom*).

Chris Cross 10 (*Bottom left*); 11; 48 (*Bottom right*).

Daemmrich 160 (*Top*).

David M. Doody 25 (*Bottom right*); 32; 33 (*Bottom left*); 70 (*Bottom right*); 81 (*Top*); 126 (*Bottom left*); 134 (*Bottom*); 147 (*Top*).

Hugo Fast 33 (*Bottom left*).

Charles Feil 13 (*Bottom*); 33 (*Top right*); 84 (*Bottom*); 117; 139 (*Bottom*); 169 (*Bottom*); 174 (*Bottom right*).

Jon Feingersh 13 (*Top*); 60 (*Bottom*).

W. B. Folsom 48 (*Bottom left*); 57 (*Bottom left*); 70 (*Bottom left*); 143 (*Bottom right*); 161 (*Bottom*).

Freeman 164 (*Top*).

Henley & Savage 102 (*Top right*).

C. M. Highsmith 80 (*Bottom*); 128/129; 177 (*Top*).

Everett Johnson 103

Henryk T. Kaiser 42/43; 72.

Sue Klemens 31 (*Top*); 46/47; 57 (*Bottom right*); 65 (*Top*); 70 (*Top*).

Stuart Krasner 182 (*Top right and bottom left*).

Dany Krist 2/3; 68 (2); 76 (*Top*); 77 (*Bottom*); 106; 114 (*Bottom left*); 115; 122 (*Bottom*); 124/125; 135 (*Bottom left*); 158 (*Top*); 164 (*Bottom right*).

Gary Landsman 60 (*Top*).

Wendy Ledis 36; 102 (*Top left*).

Carol Lee 126 (*Bottom right*).

R. Lee 14 (*Top*); 170 (*Bottom left*).

Regis Lefebure 179 (*Top*).

Llewellyn 16/17; 19; 26/27; 28 (*Bottom*); 29 (*Top*); 52 (*Bottom*); 58/59; 62/63; 73; 74 (*Top*); 76 (*Bottom right*); 77 (*Top*); 78/79; 82/83; 85; 96 (*Bottom*); 112/113; 120/121; 130 (*Bottom right*); 143 (*Top*); 145; 146; 150 (*Bottom left*); 154 (*Bottom left*); 159;165; 180/181.

Max Mackenzie 30 (*Top*); 71; 92 (*Bottom*); 119 (*Bottom*); 150 (*Top left*); 175 (*Top*).

Jim McGinniss 110 (*Top*).

Les Moore 28 (*Top*); 64 (*Top*); 74 (*Bottom*); 84 (*Top left*); 119 (*Top*); 151(*Top*); 164 (*Bottom left*); 191 (*Top*).

John Neubauer 135 (*Bottom right*); 182 (*Bottom right*).

Larry Olsen 10 (*Bottom right*); 90/91; 96 (*Top*); 104 (2); 111 (*Top*);138 (*Bottom* left*); 158 (*Bottom*); 166/167; 175 (*Bottom*); 191 (*Bottom*).

M. J. Pettypool 12 (*Top left*); 49 (*Top*); 81 (*Bottom left*); 100/101; 126 (*Top*);143 (*Bottom left*); 150 (*Top right*).

Stacy Pick 102 (*Bottom*); 105 (*Bottom*); 108/109; 174 (*Top left*); 190 (*Bottom*).

Carl Purcell 10 (*Top*).

M. S. Reinstein 45 (*Top*); 53; 56; 127.

Judy G. Rolfe 162/163; 186 (*Bottom*).

Martin Rogers 25 (*Top*); 66 (*Top*); 98 (*Bottom*); 130 (*Bottom left*).

Lawrence Ruggeri 132/133.

Allen Russell 76 (*Bottom left*).

Allan Seeger 24 (*Top*).

Robert Shafer 1; 4/5; 6; 8/9; 18; 40; 41; 69; 189 (*Top*).

Richard Slade 24 (*Bottom*); 37; 86; 118; 138 (*Top right*).

Joe Sohm 75; 168 (*Top*).

Shaun van Steyn 7; 134 (*Top*).

M. E. Warren 114 (*Bottom right*).

Tucker Williams 15.

K. M. Wyner 12 (*Bottom*).

Teresa Zabala 80 (*Top*); 174 (*Bottom left*).